Thrown Rope

Peter Hutchinson

Thrown Rope

Essays by
Carter Ratcliff and Bill Beckley

A BLIND SPOT BOOK

PUBLISHED BY PRINCETON ARCHITECTURAL PRESS, NEW YORK

Evolution Man
(Amphibian Series)

Anguilla   2001

Hutchinson's Travels

Carter Ratcliff

Having spent the 1960s making abstract paintings, Peter Hutchinson suddenly dropped the medium in 1968 and joined those artists who were fleeing the art world for sites far from the traditional gallery. Quickly achieving prominence as a builder of earthworks, Hutchinson did much to open up the possibilities for art in the aftermath of Minimalism. A restless innovator, he has been particularly successful in reshaping the relations between language and photographic imagery. Among his recent works, I especially like *Palindrome I* (2002), which has the look of an outsized postcard. Sent to no one in particular, it is meant for all of us.

Traditionally, the message accompanying an image like this one is "Wish you were here," though in this case there may be more to it: "Hope you notice that this picture is also a symmetrical pattern, with left mirroring right." Visual symmetry becomes verbal in the palindrome that supplies the work with its subtitle: "Desserts Stressed." At first, I read "Desserts" as "Deserts," possibly because of the defoliated look of the mountain range that runs along the top of the image, above its incandescent blossoms. The desert has been stressed, I half-consciously thought, by an outbreak of color. When I saw that "Deserts" were "Desserts," I didn't know what to think. I still don't. What in the landscape of *Palindrome I* could stress a dessert? Faced with that question, I drew a blank.

Blanks occur often in Hutchinson's art. A sequence of images called *The End of Letters−T* (1970) shows a flock of pigeons eating a "T" made of breadcrumbs. When they are done, one sees only the pattern of the paving in a square in Amsterdam: a verbal if not a visual blank. Other works overflow with words. In a book called *An Alliterative Alphabet* (1993), Hutchinson assigns a page to each of the twenty-six letters. Entitled "Quicksilver," the page devoted to "Q" has a drawing of five mercury thermometers and a text that begins, "Quantum question quite quicken quacks. 'Quails quit quotas quais quotient quills.' Quentin quacked. . ." Naturally, one tries to find a narrative, a description−something to hold on to in this current of language. Failing, one watches familiar meanings jostle and annul one another, leaving a field of intelligibility: another kind of blankness.

Though his variations on blankness all originate in Minimalism, Hutchinson did not go through a Minimalist stage, unlike Robert Smithson, Dennis Oppenheim, and others of his generation. Until late in the 1960s, Hutchinson painted abstractions of the sort he later dismissed as "mannerist." In his view, the first half of the twentieth century was the era of modernist heroes. Piet Mondrian is exemplary, the inventor of a clear, confident style in the service of a utopian vision. After that vision failed—as it did, decisively, in the aftermath of the Second World War—modernist painters could offer little more than increasingly desperate and frivolous variations on pre-war precedents. Once grand, abstraction had become precious and, to borrow one of Hutchinson's words, "hysterical."[1] To banish hysteria, he stopped painting and became an artist of a kind for which there was, in those days, no agreed-upon name.

On a trip to the Caribbean island of Tobago in 1969, Hutchinson strung five calabashes on a twelve-foot length of rope. Then he swam out to a coral reef and dove, rope in hand. Underwater, he affixed both ends of the rope to the reef. On its own, a calabash will float. Rising toward the surface, unable to reach it, Hutchinson's evenly spaced calabashes drew the rope into a parabolic arc. Here, in this gracefully curving form, was an early instance of the symmetry that appeared decades later in *Palindrome I*.

Minimalist symmetry was highly visible in the late 1960s, as were reactions to Minimalism in the work of Smithson and his contemporaries. Still, it is remarkable that Hutchinson moved so quickly from the overwrought "mannerism" of his paintings to the serenity of *Threaded Calabash Underwater* and *Apple Triangle* (1970), a three-sided formation of bright yellow apples that the artist placed on a dark lava field near Mt. Paricutin, a volcano near Guadalajara, Mexico. With these early pieces, Hutchinson did two things at once: he acknowledged the significance of Minimalist geometry in all its blunt clarity, and he found ways to inflect it, to reinvent it, in places far beyond the reach of the Minimalist aesthetic. By the early 1970s, Hutchinson was a leading presence among his contemporaries—in reputation if not always in literal fact, given his love of travel.

It is often said that the plain cubes and uninflected grids of Minimalism were a reaction against Abstract Expressionism. This claim gets some support from Frank Stella, who once explained his black stripe paintings by saying he wanted "to find a way that wasn't so wrapped up in the hullabaloo"—meaning all the talk of myth and existential extremity that accompanied Abstract Expressionism at its melodramatic extremes.[2] Understood this way, Minimalism was a shift in emotional tone, from hyper to catatonic. Yet it was far more than that, and another quip by Stella helps us understand why. "What you see is what you see," he said in 1966, in the spirit of the literalist regime that he and the Minimalists had inaugurated.[3] Until then, what you saw in a work of art was something more than paint on canvas or an articulated chunk of stone or metal. Paintings pictured people and things. Statues bodied them forth. But a Minimalist object did nothing of the sort. Simply being whatever it self-evidently was, it showed that art need not be representational. It need not express anything. Minimalism dispensed with ideas taken as essential to the very idea of art by everyone from Plato to Harold Rosenberg, champion of the Abstract Expressionist "action painter."

The Minimalist object needed only a few seasons to establish its salient characteristics. At its bluntest, it was constructed of straight lines, right angles, and flat planes. So were the galleries where the Minimalists showed their work. Condensing right-angled space into right-angled objects, Minimalism was in self-evident synch with its white-walled world. Blankness had expanded from object to environment and everything simply was what it was. This literalism liberated certain younger artists, yet it baffled them as well, for it didn't offer any obvious way forward. What could one do but take a step backward to expression or representation?

Hutchinson jokes about the second option in a detail from *The Paradox of the Twins* (1976). With four photographs of himself crouching beside a large sheet of silvered glass, the artist gives a literal demonstration of the ancient and still persistent notion that representation is mirroring. This literalism generates symmetry as well, in the relationship between Hutchinson's face and its reflection. And the cruciform arrangement of the four images is also symmetrical. But just a moment, one might say—doesn't Hutchinson employ various kinds of representation throughout his oeuvre? Why would he make fun of it here?

The answer, I think, is that he is not making a joke at the expense of representation itself. His target is the sort of theory about representational art that depends too heavily on the metaphor of the mirror. With drawings, photographs, and fragments of stories, Hutchinson does indeed represent a variety of subjects. But he does so with an oblique wit, with a playfulness that opens rather than narrows the field of possibility. So the point of his art is rarely to be found in a one-to-one relationship between a representation and its subject. Meaning appears in the gaps between image and text, body and landscape, speculation and memory.

Artists of Hutchinson's generation could have replayed the Minimalist reciprocity of object and environment, artwork and gallery, but they considered that option just as pointless as a return to traditional kinds of representation. The solution was to break out of the gallery, taking along the blunt, symmetrical clarity of Minimalist form. Robert Smithson sent a 1,500-foot jetty spiraling into the Great Salt Lake in Utah. In Nevada, Michael Heizer carved two immense notches into the opposing walls of a canyon. As we have seen, Peter Hutchinson escaped to the Caribbean.

He was joined on this trip by Dennis Oppenheim, who marked the surface of the sea with a line of red dye. At first this line mimicked the contours of the highway running along the coast of Tobago—much as the Minimalist object mimicked the geometry of the white-walled gallery. Soon the dye lost its linear clarity, filling the sea with a cloud of red. Midway through this process of disintegration, Oppenheim lit patches of gasoline he had placed at intervals along his red line, and fire leapt up from the water.

Taking a less confrontational attitude toward the sea, Hutchinson displaced symmetry from the Minimalist object to a string of tropical gourds—from the rigid certainties of the gallery space to a sea stirred by tides and rip currents. The question is: so what? Why does it matter that the Minimalists dismissed traditional composition in favor of symmetry and serial repetition? More important, what did Hutchinson accomplish by inducing these formal devices to thrive in habitats far from the confines of the art gallery?

Too often, we simply trace the way form evolved, as if a pattern of evolution were a kind of revelation. But it never is. Form needs to be interpreted, and we can't begin to make sense of symmetry until we glimpse the meanings of the option it replaced. Before Minimalism, symmetry was considered suitable only for the simpler branches of the decorative arts. The fine arts of painting and sculpture required composition: the harmonious thrust and counter-thrust of disparate forms. Think of *contrapposto* in Michelangelo's *David* or the swirling energies Tiepolo brings into balance in his larger canvases. Major modernists—Braque and Picasso, Matisse and Mondrian—made composition itself a subject of art. This was no mere exercise in form, for composition—visual, musical, literary—has a crucial significance in our culture: subordinating small elements to large, it idealizes hierarchy. Thus a successful composition makes a symbolic argument in favor of traditional authority. Replacing composition with symmetry and the serial repetition of identical forms, the Minimalists rejected hierarchy. So Minimalism was, among other things, an argument for the unqualified equality of absolute democracy.

Rather, an array of Minimalist cubes embodies a way of being, and it is we who make an argument about equality in making sense of Minimalist objects. Works of art are not, after all, statements or illustrations of concepts. They are gestures made in a field of precedent and possibility, complex yet mute, and thus they engage us by challenging our powers of interpretation. Certain artworks appear in tightly circumscribed fields. A monochrome painting, for example, might require us to consider only a narrow patch of recent art history (though it seems that Brice Marden wants us to think of Velazquez as well as Ad Reinhardt when we look at his gray-green slabs of pigment from the early 1970s). However that may be, it is certain that Minimalism's leveling of hierarchy persuaded Hutchinson that the field of art is boundless. To cohere, a composition needs a firm boundary, hence the traditional importance of the frame. Symmetry, which is so easily repeated, and seriality, which *is* repetition, require no frame, imply no limits. For Hutchinson, the traveler, the possibilities of art are as wide as the world.

While he was in Tobago, Hutchinson executed a variation on *Threaded Calabash Underwater* called *Arc* (1969). Having filled a dozen bags with bits of chopped-up calabash, he bound them at regular intervals to a fifty-foot length of rope. Next, he attached the rope to the reef, where it lay inert until the calabashes began to decompose. As carbohydrates turned gaseous, the bags ascended and another parabola appeared. *Threaded Calabash Underwater* and *Arc* might be called works of process art. Thinking of Hutchinson beneath the surface of the Caribbean, grappling with pieces of rope, one might be tempted to call him a performance artist. Near the site of *Arc*, Hutchinson found what he called "a small underwater canyon." Filling one end of it with sandbags, he produced a miniature dam.[4] Performance artist becomes earthworker.

On his visit to Paricutin, in Mexico—the site of *Apple Triangle*—Hutchinson threw four hundred and fifty pounds of bread into the volcano's mouth and waited for the bread to grow a crop of mold. The idea, he said, was to "juxtapose a microorganism against a macrocosmic landscape."[5] For practical purposes, we say that the setting of this work is a geographical feature of the Mexican landscape: a certain volcano. Yet there is no plausible way to frame this piece, to draw a boundary around it. Hutchinson's macrocosm is limitless—infinitely large, in contrast to the microorganisms of mold, which point toward the infinitely small. Hutchinson has a soft spot for mold. It appears in a number of his works, possibly because it evokes these spatial extremes. When Hutchinson broke out of the gallery, he addressed himself to all of space, at every scale.

Mold Sculpture (2005) is not very big, yet it has the look of an immense, craggy mountainside. *City* (1972) includes a photograph of fireweed and an ink sketch of a vertical city that borrows the forms of this modest plant and scales them up to the size of office towers and heliports. *Iceberg Project* (1969) pictures a huge chunk of ice at the narrow end of which stand tubes of earth and crystals. According to the caption, the iceberg "will eventually drift south and melt near where the Titanic sank. The tubes would remain at the sea bottom"—where, presumably, the microorganisms in the tube of earth would survive, at least for a time. *The Iceberg that Sank the Titanic Project* (1984) is a proposal for plantings of green boxwood, red barberry, and other shrubs in lines that map the *Titanic*'s collision course. Most of Hutchinson's narratives come full circle—literally so in *World Trip* (1973), a photograph of a globe marked by a black loop that traces the artist's circumnavigation of the world "by plane, train, bus, and ship, 1950/51." Hutchinson was a traveler before he became an artist, and his art can be understood as a meditation on traveling: its pleasures as well as the dangers he evokes with his allusions to the *Titanic*. Sometimes there is no return voyage. And sometimes there is not even a destination.

I mentioned earlier the verbal blank—the buzz of white noise—generated by some of Hutchinson's alliterative texts. Others raise the possibility of a narrative. See, for example, the text of *Elephant Rock* (2002): "Exercise rockclimbing exerts rapid excitement. Rarely events really exceed recovery. Each rock entails random elevation. Rushing ensures risk. Ellen rashly established rappelling, especially respected, eventually recovered." Driven by the alternation of *e* and *r*, which the artist derived from the title of this piece, these sentences seem to be going somewhere. Someone, possibly Ellen, is taking risks, feeling excitement. But just as possibly, "Ellen" is no more—or less—than a function of the circular *e-r* pattern. Though the text stops when Hutchinson runs out of space, there is in principle no reason why it should not go on forever. If it did, it still wouldn't go anywhere. Or one could say that the mock-narrative of *Elephant Rock* would eventually go everywhere: continued nonstop, the micropattern of *e* and *r* words would refer to the macrocosm of everything that exists.

To go everywhere and to go nowhere—Hutchinson's works often do both at once. One sees this doubleness in *Biological Circle* (1970), which juxtaposes roses and coal in the waters off Cape Cod. As the text notes, plants "can decay and be compressed into coal." This sounds like a one-way journey, from vegetable life to a mineral state beyond life and death. Yet coal is not entirely inert. It can burn and its carbon can come back to life, so to speak, as a constituent of a blooming plant. Whenever Hutchinson uses organic materials—mold, flowers, calabashes—he sets in motion a cycle of decay and regeneration, which can be understood as a voyage from one state to another and back again. The journey out implies the return, which leads in turn to another journey. The beginning is the end is the beginning. Thus the symmetry of a palindrome reappears in the artist's sense of the way the world hangs together.

"GOD SAW I WAS DOG/DOG SAW I WAS GOD," according to a work from 1974, which includes a photograph of a Dalmatian hound leashed to a white car, juxtaposed with another picture showing the car covered with Dalmatian spots and the hound all white. Verbal and visual, organic and inorganic—Hutchinson sees all things in cyclical flux. With his travels he joins the prevailing patterns, always bearing in mind the lesson of the *Titanic*: not every cycle finds its way to completion. And with his Thrown Ropes he establishes paths that lead in only one direction. Or that is the impression one gathers from works such as *Thrown Rope II* (1974). Here we see the artist winding up to heave a length of rope across the lawn of the Stedelijk Museum, in Amsterdam. His energy is about to convert the rope into a vector, a linear form with a head and a tail. *Thrown Rope II* also includes a photograph of the row of yellow flowers that Hutchinson planted along the path marked by the rope as it fell to the ground. This image tells us nothing about the direction in which the rope was thrown. The surging energy of this row of flowers runs, like a palindrome, both ways at once.

In a note on the Thrown Rope pieces, Hutchinson said, "They owe more to John Cage than to Duchamp in that they employ the device of selected choice. I throw the ropes more than one time (a rope might just land in a heap), and then stop when an acceptable shape is formed, which uses the accident and so is not shaped deliberately. I then plant flowers or hedges along this shape."[6] A Thrown Rope piece executed in the Hofgarten Düsseldorf in 2002, exchanges plants for bricks—shades of early works by the Minimalist Carl Andre, who sent rows of bricks across gallery floors. There are, of course, differences. Andre's lines were ruler-straight. Hutchinson's meander in wide arcs, with occasional zigzags. It is not just that he permits contingencies to inflect his clarities—he invites them to do so. Gravitational happenstance shapes his Thrown Ropes. Biological processes, working on their own, determine the fate of those works which incorporate mold, apples, and other varieties of vegetable matter. Sometimes the weather gets in on the act.

In 1972 he produced *Hyacinth Thrown Rope* on the grounds of the Krefeld Museum, in Germany. Hutchinson's caption to his photograph of this red and white configuration recalls that, while he worked on the piece, he lived on the museum grounds in an apartment reserved for artists. "Some nights," he says, "I had to protect the flowers with covers as it became frosty." In response to a chill in the air, the artist must take action. Of course, even the most delicate pencil drawing—think of Watteau—requires action of a kind. Nonetheless, by dispensing with the skills required for traditional representation, Minimalism opened the way for artists to act in ordinary, down-to-earth ways. Building, excavating, or simply walking through the streets, they became earthworkers, process artists, performance artists. At various points in his career, each of those labels has applied to Hutchinson.

Always, though, he has been on the move, actually or metaphorically, which means that some variation on the idea of travel is applicable to his entire oeuvre. One cannot make sense of Hutchinson's outdoor pieces without thinking of him journeying to Mexico to climb up the side of a volcano, or to Europe, where he heaves a length of rope and plants a row of hyacinths or crocuses. *Foraging* (1970), which exists as a film and as a series of photographic stills, records a hike of six days through some very rough terrain in the Rocky Mountains of Colorado. As the author of these works, he is a robustly physical presence. In the vicinity of his alliterative texts, he becomes a bit ghostly. One imagines a mind pressured by the rules of the game to come up with one word after another, all starting with the same letter or with the same pair of letters, as in *Elephant Rock*.

Hutchinson recently described this sort of composition as his version of automatic writing, the originally Surrealist procedure that was intended to tap directly into the unconscious. As I've suggested, Hutchinson uses alliteration to induce words to drift away from their familiar meanings, even when he enforces a further rule: the verbal sequences cannot be incoherent; they must form sentences, no matter how bewildering.[7] Hutchinson commemorated the difficulty of living up to his own demands in a work called *Struggling with Language* (1974). Here mind becomes body as the artist grapples with a swarm of large metal letters. Yet language is not always rough going. Sometimes the artist's texts sound like fragments of a perfectly intelligible travel diary.

The four photographs in *Winter Work* (1999) show apples arranged in triangles–a reprise of *Apple Triangle*, from nearly three decades earlier. The caption explains, "When spending a week in Villiers, as I do each Christmas, I try to find something to occupy myself. Collecting late apples is one such thing." *Four-Part Thrown Rope–Venice Biennale* (1980) consists of a drawing of the work; a photograph of its installation, with blossoms of various colors; and a note, "This work, in front of the American pavilion, was destroyed by a violent hailstorm just as the American ambassador was leaving the building. It was rebuilt (instructions by telephone) but with white flowers." Anecdotes like these began to appear in Hutchinson's art during the early 1970s. At the time, he was leading a trend toward "Story Art," to quote the title of a 1973 exhibition at the John Gibson Gallery, in New York.

As James Collins, another story artist, wrote the following year, the label "covers a wide range of artists who *welcome* rather than reject a story element in their art, be it visual or verbal."[8] Other members of this loosely knit group were Bill Beckley and Mac Adams. All of them saw the symmetry and blankness of Minimalism as liberating but inadequate. Determined to fill this void, they presented narrative fragments one after another, as in the serial arrangements of Minimalist installations. Disrupting the flow of traditional storylines–much as visual symmetries disrupt the harmonies of traditional composition–this fragmentation calls into question the coherence we habitually impose on events: the Aristotelian pattern of beginning, middle, and end. With bits and pieces of that pattern, Hutchinson invokes the possibility of a traditional narrative and then overwhelms it with contingencies or expands it into a cycle that makes it impossible to tell where it begins or ends. Or he does both at once.

His *Alphabet Series* (1974) consists of twenty-six panels, one for every letter from A to Z. Each panel presents a capital letter, a photograph, and a handwritten text. On the first, an aluminum "A" is centered above a photograph of a wooden chair. On its seat sits an artichoke and a bowl containing an apple. Below is an account of a night the artist spent in an Italian artichoke field, on his way to a visit with friends. Some time before dawn, he hears the nearby rustling of an unidentified creature. Mildly apprehensive, he moves his sleeping bag a few yards off, crawls back in, and goes to sleep.

The recurrence of things starting with "A" gives this initial panel a certain coherence. As one accompanies Hutchinson through the alphabet to Z, certain characters appear and reappear—Horace and Holly, especially—and one comes to rely on the calm tone and oblique drift of the artist's quasi-narratives. There is continuity as well in the repetition of the first panel's three-part configuration. As Collins noted, this arrangement "shows Minimalism's influence, yet there's none of its abstraction . . . the written stories under the pictures condition the way you look at them. Stories also suggest what abstract artists try so hard to avoid: a real-life context with a possible past, present, and future."[9]

Two Rhodes Works (1999) commemorates several of Hutchinson's trips to the island of Rhodes. Combining pictures from 1974 and 1980 with texts written in 1980 and 1999, this work has the feel of a scrapbook. *Rhodes Works* may or may not be a pun on "road works"; clearly, however, there is a pun intended by the juxtaposition of two photos: one of the sole of a foot and the other of a large, flat cactus leaf with five small, toelike leaves at its outer edge. There is an unresolved story about Hutchinson visiting Bill Beckley in a house on Rhodes and eating too many figs from a tree in the garden. Elsewhere, two pictures of the artist in a pirate costume flank a picture of the Parthenon. This array is entitled *The Colossus of Rhodes*. Or, asks the subtitle, "is it Gulliver's Travels?"

No, the travels are all Hutchinson's, though his allusion to Jonathan Swift's wandering hero makes a helpful point in a characteristically roundabout way. Swift planned Gulliver's travels to provide him with satiric leverage against all the offenses and abuses he perceived in eighteenth-century England. Hutchinson left twentieth-century England when he was young because he felt a need, as he has said, to be "the foreigner."[10] Perennially foreign but never alien, his travels keep him alert to the grand cycles and minuscule subtleties of weather and the seasons, of decay and regeneration. In his art, symmetries make those cycles vivid. When they are disrupted, the contingencies of the artist's life come into focus—as does the resourcefulness and wit with which he engages the world's vagaries.

Hutchinson has often been a solitary traveler. *Writer's Block* (2005), shows half a dozen pencils frozen into a block of ice. Behind this rueful sculpture is a panel covered with scraps of paper, one of which reads, "If you had been there I should have been pleased." "You" may be someone in particular or anyone who happens to reads these words. Learning from Minimalism how to endow form of every sort with complete equality, Hutchinson has spent decades applying that lesson in the world beyond the art gallery—though not, of course, in a didactic spirit. His egalitarian openness comes across in the record of his travels, real and imaginary. Endlessly responsive—the Thrown Ropes, for instance, are salutations to the very fact of space—his art is the product of life lived with indefatigable attentiveness to the world we all inhabit and often barely notice. Bringing our world to our attention, Hutchinson invites us to make of it what we will. Like any true egalitarian, he assigns us full responsibility for ourselves, and his works show us, with remarkable generosity, how rich the exercise of this responsibility can be.

Notes

1   Peter Hutchinson, "Mannerism in the Abstract," in Gregory Battcock, ed. *Minimalism: An Anthology* (New York: E. P. Dutton, 1968), 187-94.

2   William S. Rubin, *Frank Stella*, exhibition catalog (New York: The Museum of Modern Art, 1970), 12-13.

3   Frank Stella, in Bruce Glaser, "Questions to Stella and Judd" (1966), in Battcock, ed. *Minimalism*, 158.

4   Peter Hutchinson, conversation with the author, June 15, 2000, New York.

5   Peter Hutchinson, quoted in Lucy Lippard, *Six Years: The Dematerialization of the Art Object from 1966 to 1972* (New York: Praeger, 1973), 95, 145.

6   Peter Hutchinson, "Notes on Thrown Ropes Pieces." Unpublished statement, 2005.

7   Peter Hutchinson, conversation with the author, April 3, 2005.

8   James Collins, "Story Art," in *New York Magazine* (October 28, 1974): 21.

9   Ibid.

10   Peter Hutchinson, conversation with the author, April 3, 2005.

Lime Line

A fifty-foot line drawn in lime
on the beach at Provincetown. The
sea came in to cover it. (Returning
calcium carbonate to the sea.)

1969

GRASS LIME PIECE

Lime, grass seed, grass over several
months 1969/70, Provincetown - approx. 30 ft.
This path is now a road - Aunt Sukie's Way

ARC

In thirty feet of sea water in the Caribbean off Tobago. Bags of molding chopped calabash on rope.

1969

SPIDER

7 ft diameter. Sand, sea weed on tar.
Long Island beach.   1969

RESTRICTED GROWTH

Anacharis weed in glass tube in a
fish tank, with guppy.   1968

ICEBERG PROJECT

collage of an idea for tubes of earth
and crystals for an iceberg which
will eventually drift south and melt
near where the Titanic sank. The
tubes would remain at the sea bottom.

1969

The Iceberg that sank the Titanic
Project

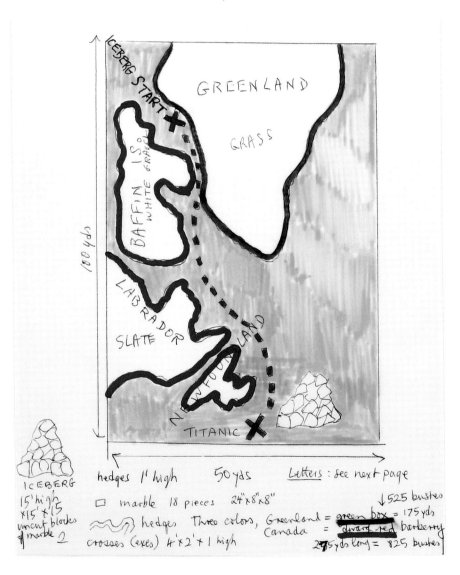

hedges 1' high   50 yds   <u>Letters</u>: see next page

☐ marble 18 pieces 24"x8"x8"

〜〜 hedges Three colors, Greenland = green box = 175 yds

crosses (exes) 4'x2'x1 high   Canada = ~~dwarf red~~ barberry

ICEBERG

15' high
x15' x15'
uncut blocks
of marble 2

↓525 bushes

275 yds long = 825 bushes

1984

LONG POINT PROJECT
(COMPLETED JULY 22, 1969)
(FOURTH MOLD LINE PIECE)

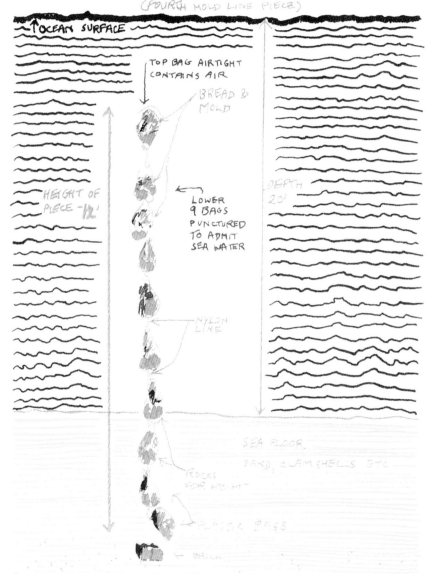

OCEAN SURFACE

TOP BAG AIRTIGHT
CONTAINS AIR

BREAD & MOLD

HEIGHT OF PIECE - 12'

DEPTH 20'

LOWER 9 BAGS PUNCTURED TO ADMIT SEA WATER

NYLON LINE

SEA FLOOR
SAND, CLAMSHELLS ETC

ROCKS FOR WEIGHT

PLASTIC BAGS

DRILL

PROVINCETOWN, Mass.

PROJECT FOR TOBAGO

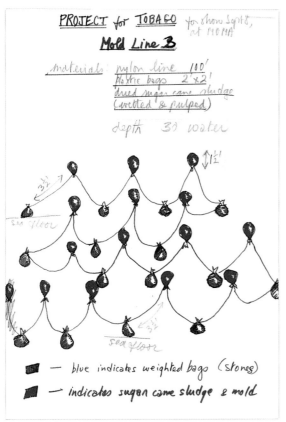

PROJECT for TOBAGO *for show Sept 8, at MOMA*

Mold Line 3

materials: nylon line 100'
plastic bags 2'×2'
dried sugar cane sludge
(wetted & pulped)

depth 3' water

◊ 1½'

3' ↗

sea floor

3' ↗

sea floor

■ — blue indicates weighted bags (stones)

◆ — indicates sugar cane sludge & mold

drawing for project 1969

realized in 1996, but
in St. Barts, W.I.

Sulphur Piece

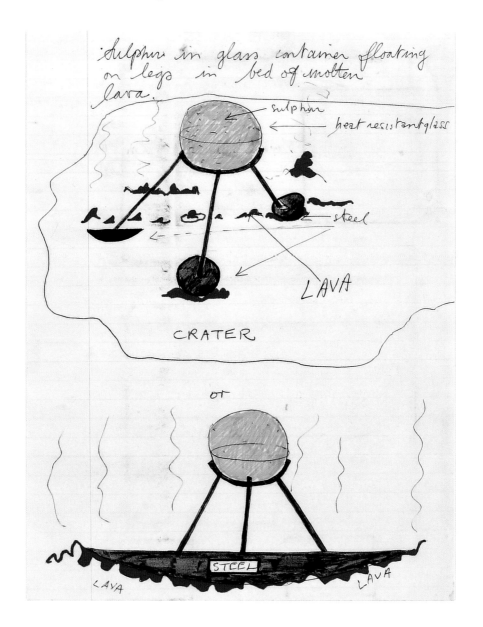

Sulphur in glass container floating
on legs in bed of molten
lava.

sulphur

heat resistant glass

steel

LAVA

CRATER

or

LAVA   STEEL   LAVA

March 10, 1969

APPLE TRIANGLE

done at Mt. Paricutin, Mexico in 1970
in a field of lava

triangle
six ft.
on each
side

1970

UNDERSEA FLOWER TRIANGLE

Flowers placed in sand in shallow
water at Tobago.

1969

Biological Circle

Undersea, off Long Point, Cape Cod.
A circle of coal and roses. Organic
origins can decay and be compressed
into coal.   1970

UNDER SEA ARC of ORANGES

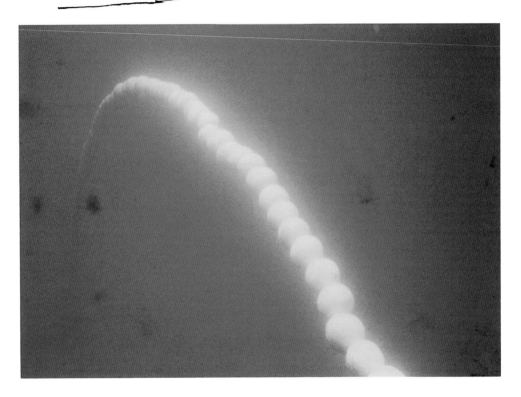

Provincetown harbor   1970

Floating Bricks

Plan

completed project

Bricks suspended
by balloons at
breakwater, Provincetown
in 7ft of seawater.

Summer 1979

UNDERSEA ONIONS

Provincetown breakwater   1970

MUSSELS AND MUSHROOMS

Cape Cod beach at low tide with
mussels and oyster mushrooms.

1970

FORAGING

(A hike of six days in the Snowmass
Wilderness as a work of art.)

Also done as a super 8 film.

1970

Paricutin Volcano Project

450 lbs. of crumbled bread laid out on
the edge of the crater, approx. 250 feet
long. After six days, with the help
of heat and steam from the volcano,
mold appeared. (see left side of
crater on photo)

Mexico 1970 (Jan)

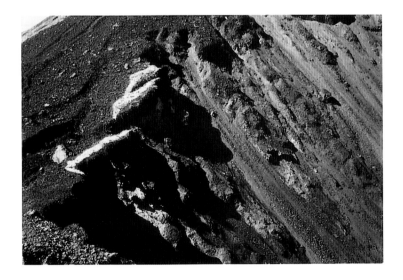

LLAMA

Mexico 1971

approx 30ft x 10ft
lime on lava dust

CHRYSANTHEMUM DIAMOND

36" x 21 3/4"
photo.
collage & drawing
S. England 1971

My mother Linda drove the getaway car.
I was approached by a polite English
policeman who inquired whether I had
seen anyone stealing cabbages.

Star

Plan for tulip
field, Holland,
to cut down
the tulips in
order to get this
shape.
collage photo, ink
1971

(not completed)

MOLD WALL

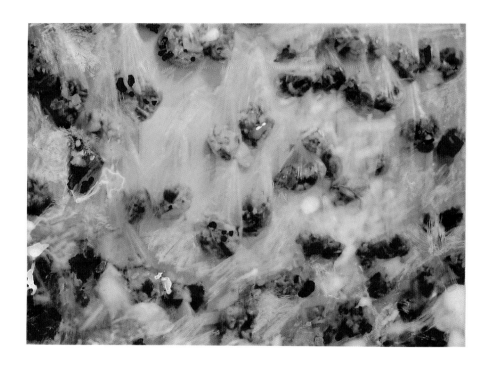

Hanging wall of bread mold in plastic bags
at Galerie Fenna de Vries, Rotterdam.
(hand colored)

(I could not stay long enough to see the
true colors of the molds appear.)

1971

MUSHROOMS AND MOLDS

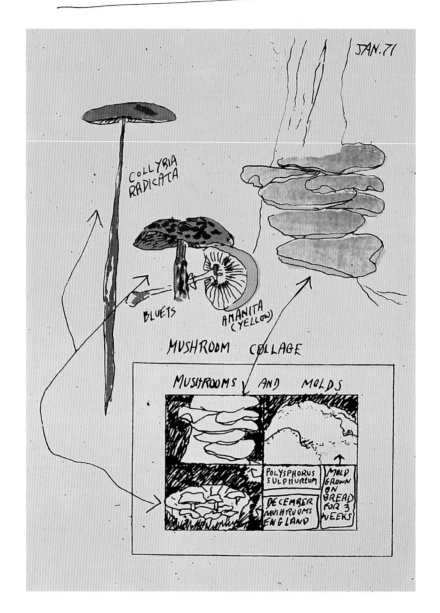

JAN. 71

COLLYBIA RADICATA

BLUETS

AMANITA (YELLOW)

MUSHROOM COLLAGE

MUSHROOMS AND MOLDS

POLYSPHORUS SULPHUREUM

DECEMBER MUSHROOMS ENGLAND

MOLD GROWN ON BREAD FOR 3 WEEKS

drawing on paper and plan for photo collage.

CITY

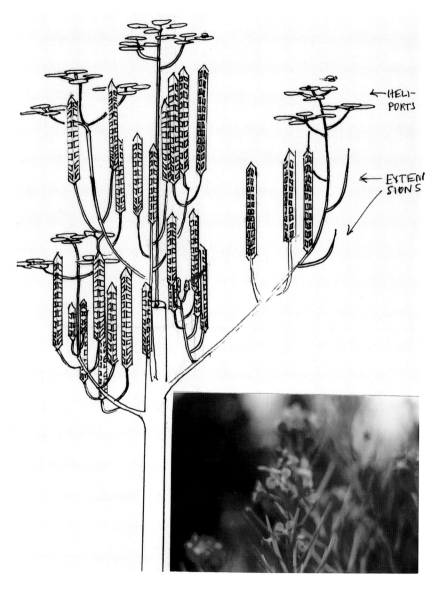

← HELI-
PORTS

← EXTEN-
SIONS

idea for a city based on fireweed.
1972

WORLD TRIP

Circumnavigating the world by plane,
train, bus and ship, 1950/51

(Detail from "The Anarchist's Story" series, 1973)

BEACH ZEBRA

Zebra specially adapted to be
invisible near the sea.   1974
                                    serigraph
                                    of drawing & photo

detail from

GOD SAW I WAS DOG
DOG SAW I WAS GOD

1974

Coastal Tubes

Collage: tube sculptures on the
Mediterranean coast at Ramatuelle, France

1975

HANGING GARDEN

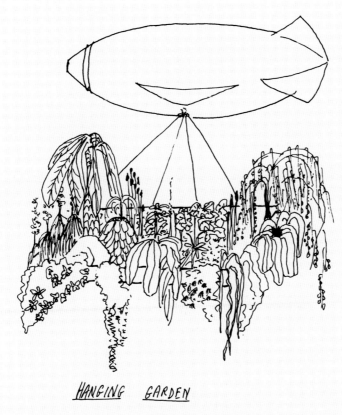

HANGING GARDEN

that can be moved with the seasons

proposal fort the 8th wonder of the world

1983

(from the book "Projects,"
Michael Erloff, publisher)

COLOR SEQUENCE

(a permanent structure with some
impermanent parts)

105"

|(BLACK METAL EDGE)

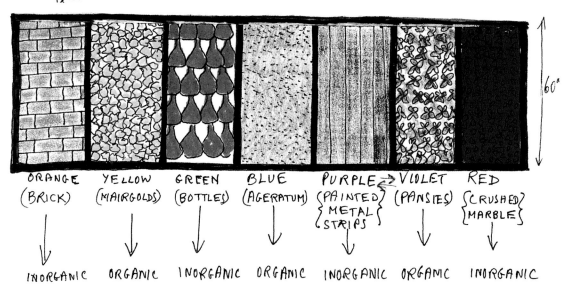

60"

ORANGE   YELLOW   GREEN   BLUE   PURPLE→VIOLET   RED
(BRICK) (MAIRGOLDS) (BOTTLES) (AGERATUM) (PAINTED) (PANSIES) {CRUSHED}
                                {METAL   {MARBLE}
                                {STRIPS

INORGANIC ORGANIC INORGANIC ORGANIC INORGANIC ORGANIC INORGANIC

1983

(from the book "Projects,"
Michael Erloff, publisher)

RAINBOW CIRCLE

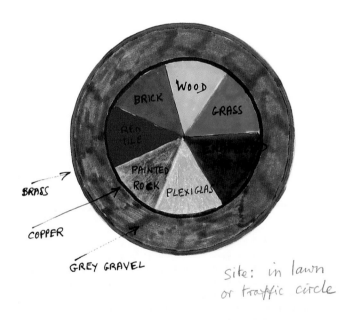

BRICK

WOOD

GRASS

RED TILE

PAINTED ROCK

PLEXIGLAS

BRASS

COPPER

GREY GRAVEL

site: in lawn
or traffic circle

installation project

1984

Citrus Freeze

1980

Thinking of the tropics during a long, cold winter.

The sea froze on P'Town beaches. It was so cold that I only completed this piece with the help of a few drinks of brandy.

ICE SANDWICH

Ice from my wild cat's drinking
bowl over four days in winter.

1994

SHOAL BEACH PROJECT

1996

at Shoal Bay, Anguilla
with helper in approx.
15 ft. of water.

RAINBOW   WALL

Collage of photos and glazed enamel bricks.
Soon to be constructed as a wall of bricks.

1997

SWAMP
TRIANGLE

soapwort flowers
in Provincetown
swamp with
water lilies.

October 1970

Reconstituted Palms

July 1999

Old wharf pilings, Provincetown harbor.

Down and Up

Twenty-one years ago
I hitch-hiked into
Paris, became sick and
went to the hospital
at Cité Universitaire.
When they released me
I only had enough
money for my ticket
back to England. And
then I lost the ticket.
The British Embassy
sent me back, after
taking away my pass-
port. This year I
flew into Paris and
sold two works to
collectors, one for
$1,200. This time it
looked as though they
were tearing Paris
down. But to me that
wasn't the only dif-
ference.

Paris, 1973

Living Room

For a part of every winter, I live with Glenn, Pauline, Phlips, Emily, Carl the canary and the Fruit Juicer. Every day we make fruit and vegetable juice. One day I drank a whole cabbage. I also found out that it's impossible to make a drinkable juice from banana peel, raw potatoes, leeks, grapefruit and orange peel and tomatoes. I know. I tried it one night when there was nothing else. The living room table is usually crowded with plates of bean sprouts, hyacinths, fruit, games, food and budding art works. At least that's where I work when everybody has gone to bed. Glenn works upstairs in his studio. We all hope one day to buy a small farm in North Holland and make a barn into a studio for us.

February, 1973

detail from <u>PARADOX OF THE TWINS</u>

from "The Anarchist's Story" series.

1976

HUNTER

1978

"STRUGGLING WITH LANGUAGE"
THE ALPHABET SERIES

Provincetown   1974

"End of Letters" – "T"

THE LETTER "T" FROM
THE SUPER-8 MOVIE
"THE END OF LETTERS"
IN WHICH THE LETTERS
FROM THE WORDS THE
END ARE EACH DES-
TROYED IN A DIFFERENT
MANNER. THIS "T" IS
MADE FROM BREAD
CRUMBS EATEN BY PIG-
EONS AT DAM SQUARE,
AMSTERDAM.

"E" from "The End of Letters"

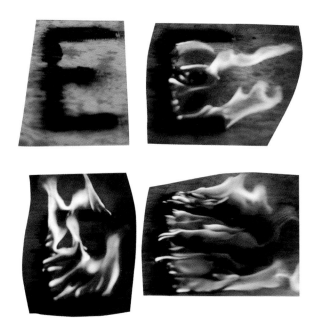

materials: tar on wood
(the whole series of disappearing letters
contained in the title THE END OF LETTERS
is dated 1971-80)

"V" FROM THE ALPHABET SERIES

also done as super-8 film

1974

NARRATIVE ART

lime letters
photographed
in different
locations in
New England

Narratives were originally stories
collected by traveling through
different landscapes and talking
to people.
1977

from the "YEAR" series. 60"x80" color photos 1978

MARCH WINDS

Sculpture of copper and aluminium
in my garden.   Winter   1982

and ideas

Drawing made for the book of that name.

1983

(from the book 'Projects,'
Michael Erloff, publisher)

TRANSFORMATION

Construction and installation at John
Gibson Gallery made from marble chips,
yew hedge and wood. Inorganic transformed
into organic.

30 ft. × 2 ft. 1987

GARDEN LITERATURE
(for D.H. Lawrence)

2002

Winter view in my garden.
Temporary, like winter.

HYACINTH THROWN ROPE

At Haus Lange, Krefeld Museum, Germany

While preparing this piece and the show in the Museum I lived in the artists' apartment at the Haus Lange. Some nights I had to protect the flowers with covers as it became frosty.

1972

THROWN ROPE II   (STEDELIJK)
                    MUSEUM

in connection with my exhibition in one room at this museum. I offered
to make the piece permanent as a hedge but was turned down.

at the Stedelijk Museum, Amsterdam   approx 20ft
                                        1974

FOUR-PART THROWN ROPE – VENICE BIENNALE

1980

drawing plan

approx.
30 ft × 30 ft

This work, in front of the American pavilion, was destroyed by a violent hailstorm just as the American ambassador was leaving the building. It was rebuilt (instructions by telephone) but with white flowers.

Lawn Stripe

lime, paint, grass   30ft x 6ft
(my garden)   1984

ROSE BRIDGE

Rose Bridge Plan
for Weimar Artists'
Garden

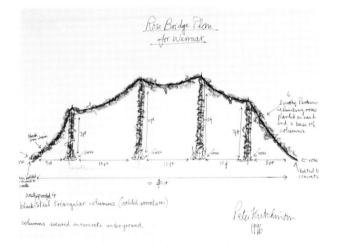

Although this was never built
at the Bauhaus Universität, the
students made a charming
mock-up of it for my lecture
appearance.

TEENY AND THE APPLE SEMI-CIRCLE

Teeny, Gauguin and I inspecting
my Apple Semi-Circle.

1992

Ghost Thrown Ropes

size: approx.
20 ft x 8 ft.
yew hedge &
crocus 1996

The word ghost
refers to the
fact that crocus
completely
disappear after
flowering, to
return the
following spring.

Thrown Ropes at Künstler-Gaarten, Weimar,
Bauhaus Universität, Weimar, Germany
photo: Barbara Nemitz 1999

THROWN ROPE LIGHTS

in my garden at night, winter
2003

Candide

In my own search for perfection, notably absent from my life, I have always been drawn to Switzerland. The purity of sea birds and horses (from Bermuda) have the rarefied quality of the air from the highest mountains.

photo-collage, oilstick,   40"x 54"   1996
ink, text

Gloire de Dijon
(Alliterative Landscape Series)

Good direction describes generous
dynamics. Despite gerotic develop-
ments, deep, glorious, dependable,
defined groups defend double
generation. Definitely dilated,
greatly durable, densiably glabrous.

photo-collage, oil stick,
ink, text   60"x40" 1998

Exploding Forest Landscape
Hexagonal Series II

2000 40"x40"
photo-collage

Australian Dream

My friend Billy went to Australia and found my father, whom I had not seen since childhood, nor remembered. Although this meeting did not result in a reunion, somehow I made a connection with Australia, hence the Australian swans.

photo-collage, crayons, ink, text

40"x60"
2001

Arp Thrown Rope

At Rolandseck, Germany, I went on a
long walk looking for an ancient
volcano. I think I found it, an
unimpressive mound & small depression
covered in wild flowers. Then I became
lost and didn't find my way back
or anyone to ask directions for four
hours. A german friend remarked: "You
cannot walk for four hours in this part
of the country without coming across a
village. So I had to conclude that I
had been walking very slowly.

2001 40"x60"

Photo collage, text, crayon

Arp Thrown Rope

Approx. 50ft x 50ft., rocks, hedge, flowers
on the banks of the river Rhine in
Remagen, Germany commissioned
by the Arp Museum Rolandseck

2001 July

Last Tango

(Alliterative Botanical Series)

Let time dlinger, tempests last.
Triumphal clabors take lost total
latitude. Torrential loving truly
leaves touth.

photo collage, text

30"x 40"
2001

Coma Berenice

(Alliterative Botanical Constellations)

Come, bring comestibles, buy
convertibles but carry brochures.
Could be, character belies con-
ditions. Better confirm before
combining because counting
beats courting. Besides, clues
bracket causes.

photo-collage, text   40"x60"
                                        2002

Clair de Lune
(Alliterative Landscape Series)

Constant determination lets creatures
do limitless conversions. Denying
life's conventions does lengthen
character, defines logic, confirms
details. Likewise, conversation
demonstrates literacy. Clair de
lune can determine life's definitions.

photo-collage, watercolor pen,
ink, text   40"x60" 2002

PALINDROM 1

Desserts   Stressed

photo·collage, colored crayon, ink, text

Canadian Dream

I once had the desire to live in the back-
woods of Canada but somehow finished
up living 22 years in New York City.

2003

photo collaage
text

30" x 40"

Lemon Soufflé
(Giant Flower Series)

An afternoon at the Café Blasé

photo-collage, text   30"x40"   2003

THE EFFECT OF GAMMA RAYS

photo, watercolor collage

2003

Unfrozen Water

Years ago, while walking on the ice
of the boating pond in Central Park,
I looked down and saw a school of
golden fish swimming beneath the
frozen surface. Last winter I also
walked on the ice of the water depicted
above.

2004

photo-collage, watercolor pen,
oil stick, ink, text

60" x 40"

White Cliffs

When I grew up on the south coast of
England there were beautiful white
cliffs reaching their highest farther
west at Dover. This combination of
cliffs, Alps and my garden is a sort
of biography of my travels.

2004

photo collage, watercolor pen, 19¾" × 19¾"
oil stick, ink, text

Japanese Tree Peony
(Alliterative Giant Flower Series)

Japanese tree peonies, jewels, the
perennials, justly treasured prizes,
judged the purest June temptation.

Photo. collage, text

40" x 60"
2004

Living Variously

Bill Beckley

Although it may vex us
The garden to the world
Is the nexus
The solar plexus
   –Peter Hutchinson

Because of an apple, possibly a quince, the residents of the first garden found themselves somewhere east of Eden. Lucky for us. It was the beginning of fashion.

In the movie sequel, the evictees' metaphoric son, played by James Dean, grew beans to feed the troops during the war. His father's dissatisfaction with the legume's potential profits brought disfavor to the son, and he found himself prodigal. Voltaire had his innocent, Candide, evicted from a castle and end up in a garden. Kosinski had his innocent, Chauncey Gardiner, evicted from a garden and end up in a castle, where he would live with a woman named Eve and possibly become president.

Gardens are the starting points of civilization. In order to tend them, people had to stay in one place, build permanent housing, and thus found villages. But civilization ultimately leads to discontent. And discontent leads to repression as well as sublimation. So in gardens are the origins of art, and of everything good and ill.

A garden envelops Peter's house in Provincetown, Massachusetts. In August you have to fight your way through it to get to the front door. The sandy soil grows wild with the colors of annuals, biennials, and perennials. In their midst a stream trickles to a small pond. In its dark waters you can imagine frogs, turtles, goldfish, and snakes.

According to Peter's version of history, the first American gardeners, like himself, originally sailed from England. The Pilgrims, he told me, first landed on the tip of the Cape Cod peninsula. There the wind and sandy soil proved problematic, so they moved across the bay and settled on Plymouth. Without quite meaning to, the Puritans had founded Provincetown, now an eminent community of artists and gays.

I remember first meeting Peter in the early 1970s under a red fluorescent Flavin in the back room of Max's Kansas City. In the history of art bars, Max's comes after the Cedar Bar; by then, the hot atmosphere of Abstract Expressionism had cooled to Pop and Minimal. Max's was Andre and Andy.

By the summer of 1970, when I arrived, another crowd that included Robert Smithson, Michael Heizer, Dennis Oppenheim, and Peter, was eating Max's complimentary wings (actually, Peter may have already been a vegetarian). The chicken wings, and the Velvet Underground, attracted me to 17th and Park that night. Peter was debonair, subtle, and had a penchant for the unobtainable, and so we fast became friends forever.

This new group of artists worked outdoors. John Gibson, who became Dennis's, Peter's, and my art dealer, named this activity Earth Art. Now, it has been my contention that conceptualism, the envelope of Earth Art, Body Art, and Narrative Art, was a direct response to Minimalist painting. With a push from Clement Greenberg, painting came to be about what it was, a flat surface. Stella's flat blacks, Ryman's flat whites, Marden's flat olives, and Johns's flat reds, whites, and blues left artists without a place to go. Dave Hickey designates this flatland masculine and impenetrable, arguing that the progressive flattening of space began as far back as Velazquez. I was taught it was Manet's fault, through the ambiguous space and sexuality of *Le Déjeuner sur l'herbe*. In any case, by 1965, painterly space was as flat as it gets. In the resulting claustrophobia artists left their studios for deserts and fields, regaining space and freedom.

Richard Long picked an X of daisies in a field, and Michael Heizer dug trenches in the desert. Peter's friend Robert Smithson built a spiral jetty in Utah's Great Salt Lake. Dennis Oppenheim shoveled concentric rings in the snow of a frozen river on the Canadian border, and Peter and Dennis flew to the Caribbean and rented a rowboat to do some aquatic works. Dennis lit a ring of petrol around the boat. Peter, always one for scuba, strung a line of calabashes under water like a necklace. The Museum of Modern Art showed these and several other individual works by Dennis and Peter in 1969.

Of course, Marcel Duchamp, through his alter ego Rrose Selavy, was the grandmother of conceptual art. Like Duchamp's *Bicycle Wheel*, Smithson's *Spiral Jetty* renders a practical idea useless. The jetty sits calm in a waveless salt lake.

Peter told me he got much of his idea of chance through his friends Niki de Saint Phalle and John Cage, with whom he played chess. This element of chance is most obvious in his Thrown Rope works, an ongoing series. It is an act of selected chance, as he throws the ropes several times and chooses the best configuration, along which he plants rows of flowers. Like Cage, he is an authority on mushrooms, and often on walks in the woods near Provincetown he has plucked what seemed to me an ambiguous life-or-death mushroom out of the earth and popped it in his mouth.

Peter was also a longtime friend of Duchamp's widow, Teeny. In fact he still has the descendents of the angel wing begonias that were in her husband's studio on 14th Street when he died. Though one can't deny Duchamp's influence on the art of the late 1960s, I saw several of my classmates at art school in Philadelphia, home of the

Large Glass, destroyed by his logic of art into life. To Peter's credit, early on he had to deny Marcel Duchamp, as that other Peter denied Jesus Christ.

In 1965 racial equality, women's rights, gay rights, and the Vietnam War played much in the equation of art. The specter of the draft hung huge over that generation. And the war was a primary motivation for anti-establishment, anti-gallery art as well as Marxist aesthetics.

Marxism professed to solve the class struggle brought on by the Industrial Revolution, while Romanticism, with its emphasis on the individual and human emotions, professed to be its antidote. It was these two offshoots of the Industrial Revolution that drove factions of conceptualists in the late 1960s and early 1970s. It is probably no coincidence that David Lean directed *Dr. Zhivago* in 1965—like an earth artist, he planted thousands of daffodils around that country retreat. The film is set in a time when the schism between Romanticism and Marxism was as prevalent in Russian society as it was in the arts in America in the mid-1960s.

In the 1970s, as now, Peter and I talked mostly about the movies, science fiction in particular, and comedies on TV. That's not to say that a conversation about the movies is not about the sociopolitical events of the time. Not surprisingly, after a decade of *Cheers* and *The Mary Tyler Moore Show*, Peter's current favorite TV is reruns of *Seinfeld*, a show about "nothing." For Peter, simple transgression, that part of the human psyche that makes the off-limits meaningful—in humor as well as in human sexuality—is motivation enough. War or peace, he would have been stringing calabashes in Tobago in 1969.

In the years embracing Woodstock, photography was the mother of art. Photography made the use of other, more transient mediums possible. Like a refrigerator, it preserved the newfound working materials of art—apples, potatoes, daffodils, daisies, fire, ice.

But for most conceptualists the zone system might as well have had something to do with twilight. As documentation was a means to an end, the focus was not on technique or the craft of photography, but on the objects or installations photographed. And those objects, or more correctly anti-objects, existed within the context of painting and sculpture, not the fine art photography of Stieglitz or Minor White. Ultimately and ironically, what most people saw of Earth Art was not dirt in far off places but photographic grain in nearby galleries. Though few conceptual artists knew very much about photography, it was during their time that photography finally gained the respectability of painting. As his photo/texts evolved from documentation to fiction,

Peter was early to acknowledge the primacy of the photograph.

His texts, frivolous as they seem (there can be no greater compliment), are something apart from the work of more "serious" conceptualists. They gradually evolved from means of documentation to ends in themselves, to story for its own sake.

Actually, Peter doesn't remember meeting me that night at Max's Kansas City. He claims we first met on the occasion of the exhibition Story Art at the John Gibson Gallery on West Broadway on April 7th, 1973. Story Art was Gibson's idea too. He included Peter, John Baldessari, Italo Scanga, William Wegman, Roger Welch, David Askevold, and me in the first show. The defining link was narrative, something akin to literature, but not. Where traditional literature rarely coupled with images, Story Art always did. Prior to the printing press, monks switched from word to image with the flick of a brush. The invention of movable type made it easier to print words, but images still needed special attention. If word and image were estranged with the invention of movable type, they were reunited in some sense with Story Art. Narrative artists, and, of course, William Blake, put them back together again—as had silent film, the comics, and children's books.

With conceptual art, it was only a matter of time before documentation would turn to fiction. Story Art was a premonition of what would happen a quarter of a century later with the computer, when it would once again be so easy to switch between printed word and image.

Peter made the transition from documentation to story around the time of his *End of Letters* series. In that series the rudimentary building blocks of written language—letters—were his object.

Semiotics was a popular subject at the time. Roland Barthes, Umberto Eco, and, of course, Wittgenstein all influenced conceptual artists. But a sign is not a mirror. In representing something other than what it is, it has to have the ability to stand on its own, therefore the ability to lie. A lie is the fetus of fiction, as any ancient storyteller would know.

Whereas with Peter the shift from documentation to fiction was more of an evolution from his land art, I came to Story when, as a graduate student in 1969, I crossed the Delaware River for art at the place where George Washington crossed it for war. I didn't have the luxury of a boat, and as I crossed, dripping buckets of latex in the river, with paint and camera held above my head, I slipped and lost everything in the chilly rapids. I completed the crossing anyway, with the thought in the back of my mind (I would later call it an epiphany) that I needn't have gone to all that trouble. All that was left was the story, which I could have had in any case. It was through Story Art, common galleries, and group exhibitions, that my friendship with Peter grew.

I've already described the division among conceptualists, one camp tending toward Marxism, the other toward Romanticism. In that contest, the Marxists win, at least superficially, because by its very nature Romanticism finds fulfillment in suffering and in loss. But Thomas McEvilley thinks of those differences in another, perhaps more subtle way. For Thomas one group of conceptualists was self-referential, their art, like the Glass Bead Game in Hermann Hesse's novel, was mostly about art. The other group of conceptualists went back into the world both literally and metaphorically. I haven't asked Tom to name names, but I would imagine that Joseph Kosuth, Art and Language, Hanne Darboven, and later, Louise Lawler, tend toward the first category of conceptualists, whereas Peter is certainly of the second order—he grew mold on the rim of a volcano, for God's sake. I might add that the language of those artists loosely grouped as "Narrative" is original language; it is not the appropriated language (or language as readymade) of their more self-referential counterparts.

This cycle of art and life is never-ending. Going out to look for a real volcano is also finding Frederic Church. In the early 1800s, Thomas Cole, Church's mentor and father of the Hudson River School, read Longinus, for whom volcanoes also evoked the sublime. But Longinus was largely writing about the effects of literature, not of hot lava.

Like criminals, mushroom eaters, apple pickers, and artists define culture by crossing its borders. Of course, for criminals and mushroom eaters this is a matter of life and death. But there are different notions of transgression. Art that thrives on transgressing the rules of art (or politics or other relatively narrow pursuits) draws the circle too tight and ends up sort of like a kid who refuses to do what his father tells him just because it's what his father told him—like young George Washington chopping down a cherry tree. He doesn't necessarily end up enjoying what he's doing any more than if he simply did what he was told, though he may enjoy feeling naughty. It's a relatively negative sort of transgressing. Another sort eats the apple because he wants to taste the apple. And that's a more positive sort, to be tempted by your own serpent. It may be the only way you get out of one small garden and on to tilling another, wider one. Otherwise you're just whacking weeds, or whacking off.

But there's also something beautiful about dealing with the complexity of real living things, working in such a wide open environment. The wider the context, the more overlapping and contradictory the sets of rules. As you break one, you are inevitably weaving what remains of it into another. It's expansive rather than reductive.

This is the crux of Peter's work.

Peter was an innovator at a time when this country was in the throes of a social revolution. But Peter's revolution was personal, quiet—no rowdy demonstrations. Much has been said in postmodernism about the death of the author, as if authors were not themselves readers and alive. The simple and personal anecdotes of life that Peter has authored have become the narratives of his work, and part of the larger narrative of this time.

In an earlier revolution, Malevich's white square teetered within another white square. We don't know why it tilted that way. His answer was intuition—no logical reason, something akin to what he thought of as freedom. Unfortunately for him "revolutionaries" such as Stalin and his underlings didn't think in such a poetical fashion. Their crusty images, literal translations of social revolution, were patinaed even before they were painted. So with revolutions, sometimes we don't know what we get stuck with, except for that which is our own—something very personal.

Since I first met Peter under that red fluorescent Flavin, we've both had loves of life as well as loves of art. For a time, our generation was forgotten in the fray of the noisy market-oriented politics that followed in the 1980s, marked by Ronald Reagan, AIDS (which signified a momentary death of that 1960s sexual revolution), and Francis Ford Coppola blitzing the Woodstock generation at the end of the original *Apocalypse Now*.

But crocuses are coming up here in my garden in Kerhonkson. It was a cold and difficult winter with an almost biblical flood. (Hugh Lofting, author of *Dr. Dolittle*, about the veterinarian who conversed with animals, owned this house in the early part of the twentieth century. It feels a fitting place for one story artist to write about another in the early part of the twenty-first.) Our generation, emerging first in the 1960s, has been rediscovered recently, with museum shows in Bordeaux, Barcelona, Porto, and Kassel. It is beautifully and subtly accounted for in Carter Ratcliff's recent *Out of the Box*, amongst other books, and this.

Throughout the past forty years, Peter has worked consistently. I have never seen a break in his development, from what can be called Earth Art to what can be called

Story, to the indefinable work he is doing now. Our mutual friend and art dealer, Hans Mayer, himself an independent in an increasing massage-an-ist art world, has compared Peter to Joseph Cornell. Through his gentle poetics, Peter is enormously influential. Conceptual art is like rock and roll with a hardcore first generation, then second, third, and fourth—and, like rock and roll, it seems yet to be exhausted. Peter is one of the most significant artists of his generation, something even pre-first, as if Buddy Holly had had a predecessor.

Visiting a cemetery out in the Springs I am reminded by a stone of a poem. The stone is unobtrusive, lichen covered, lying flat in the grass a few yards away from the graves of expressionists—Jackson Pollock, Lee Krasner, and Ad Reinhart. It reads "Grace to be born and live as variously as possible." Those words well describe Peter, a life still kicking. At a time when diversity has come to mean so much of the same sameness, it's well to know Peter's work and garden. I know when he reads this he's sure to make light of everything. This is fitting, for his is the unforgettable lightness of being.

It has been said that civilization began in a garden with an act of disobedience. It may, in fact, go out with an act of obedience. And Frank O'Hara ends his poem "In Memory of My Feelings" this way:

And yet

I have forgotten my loves, and chiefly that one, the cancerous
statue which my body no longer contain,

against my will

against my love

become art,

I could not change into history

and so remember it,

and I have lost what is always and everywhere

present, the scene of my selves, the occasion of these ruses,
which I myself and singly must now kill

and save the serpent in their midst.

Contributors' Biographies

Carter Ratcliff is a poet and art critic. He is a contributing editor of *Art in America* and *Art on Paper* magazines, and is the author of *The Fate of a Gesture: Jackson Pollock and Postwar American Art* (Westview) and *Out of the Box: The Reinvention of Art 1965-1975* (Allworth Press), as well as a contributing author to *Alex Katz* (Phaidon).

Bill Beckley has exhibited extensively in Europe and America since the 1970s, with works in the permanent collections of the Whitney Museum of American Art, the Guggenheim New York, the Museum of Modern Art in New York, The Museum of Fine Arts in Boston, the Smithsonian American Art Museum in Washington, D.C., the Victoria and Albert Museum, London, and the Tate Gallery, London, as well as numerous private and corporate collections. He has edited *Uncontrollable Beauty* and *Sticky Sublime*, recent anthologies on aesthetics from Allworth Press. He teaches semiotics and literature at the School of Visual Arts in New York.

Acknowledgments

I dedicate this book to my very dear friend Rosalind Cutforth and in fond memory of Kim Zorn Caputo who first had the idea to publish this book.

Also with thanks to Virginia Dwan & Vladimir Stepczynski and James Mayor for their generous contributions. Special mention for their kind participation: ARP Museum Rolandseck, Germany; Galerie Blancpain, Stepczynski, Geneva; Galerie Bugdahn und Kaimer, Düsseldorf Frederieke Taylor Gallery, New York; The Mayor Gallery, London; Obelisk Gallery, Boston Torch Gallery, Amsterdam; Volume Gallery, New York. Also I am gratefull to: John Gibson, Teeny Duchamp, Brian O'Doherty, Nancy Holt, Robert Smithson, Al Hansen, Susan Gibson, Jackie Matisse, Holly Solomon, and many others who have helped me over the years.

My deep appreciation to Dana Faconti, Fabio Cutró and Valerie Blair at Blind Spot. I would also like to thank Scott Tennent and Nancy Eklund Later at Princeton Architectural Press for their enthusiasm, advocacy, and expertise.

Thrown Rope
Peter Hutchinson
With essays by Carter Ratcliff and Bill Beckley

A Blind Spot Book
Published by Princeton Architectural Press, New York

Blind Spot Books
210 Eleventh Avenue, 10th floor, New York, New York 10001
www.blindspot.com

Published by Princeton Architectural Press
37 East Seventh Street, New York, New York 10003

For a free catalog of books, call 1.800.722.6657
Visit our web site at www.papress.com

Art Editor: Dana Faconti
Editor: Scott Tennent
Design: Fabio Cutró and Dana Faconti / Blind Spot Photography, Inc.

Special thanks to: Nettie Aljian, Dorothy Ball, Nicola Bednarek, Janet Behning, Penny (Yuen Pik) Chu,
Russell Fernandez, Jan Haux, Clare Jacobson, John King, Mark Lamster, Nancy Eklund Later, Linda Lee,
Katharine Myers, Lauren Nelson, Jennifer Thompson, Paul G. Wagner, Joseph Weston, and Deb Wood
of Princeton Architectural Press –Kevin C. Lippert, publisher

Frontispiece: *Evolution Man,* from *Amphibian Series, Anguilla, 2001.*
Photo of Artist by Chris Pearson.

Library of Congress Cataloging-in-Publication Data

Hutchinson, Peter.
Thrown rope / Peter Hutchinson ; with essays by Carter Ratcliff and Bill Beckley.– 1st ed.
    p. cm.
  "A Blind Spot Book."
  ISBN 1-56898-561-4 (alk. paper)
1. Hutchinson, Peter–Catalogs. 2. Environment (Art)–United States–Catalogs. 3. Narrative art–United
States–Catalogs. I. Ratcliff, Carter. II. Beckley, Bill, 1946- III. Title.

  N6537.H87A4 2006
  709'.2–dc22
            2005022011